When Walls Became Wings

Elaine Dias

BookLeaf Publishing

India | USA | UK

Made with ❤ on the BookLeaf Publishing Platform
www.bookleafpub.in
www.bookleafpub.com

Dedication

To those who carried burdens too heavy for their small
shoulders,
who learned responsibility before they knew freedom,
who grew up too soon but never let the weight of the
world steal their wonder.
For the ones who find joy in quiet moments,
who turn small victories into celebrations,
who embrace the light even when shadows linger.

May you always hold onto the little things—
for in them, you have built a life of resilience, love, and
quiet magic.

Preface

There is a certain kind of childhood that feels like walking a tightrope—balancing between innocence and responsibility, between longing for care and learning to survive alone. I grew up navigating that fragile line, forced to be careful, always conscious, with little space to simply *be*. Yet, even in the weight of it all, I sought out moments of light, trying to hold onto the child I barely had the chance to be.

This collection is a reflection of that journey. A coming-of-age story woven in verses, shaped by solitude, resilience, and the search for identity. It follows the raw and unfiltered reality of growing up —navigating disappointments, questioning faith, and confronting the inevitable passage of time. But it is also a testament to hope.

When I stepped into boarding school, I found myself in an unfamiliar world—one that could have remained just another place. But I chose to let it help me, to embrace its structure, and to make it my safe haven. It became the bridge that held me together, offering me the space to grow and the stability I had long searched for. And though adulthood brings its own cages, this book is not just about struggle—it is about survival. About finding strength in self-awareness, about *reclaiming joy even in the smallest things.*

To those who have had to raise themselves, who have stitched their own wounds and carried their own weight —these words are for you. I hope the pages hold reminders of your strength, and glimpses of the hope that still remains.

Enjoy this book not just as poetry, but as a narrative—a reminder that even in solitude, we are never truly alone.

Acknowledgements

This book captures a journey I did not walk alone, even when it felt like I did. Though my path was shaped by solitude, there were moments of light—people, places, and memories that helped me hold on, even when I didn't realize it.

To my boarding school—you were more than just a place; you were my refuge, my structure, my saving grace. The lessons, the teachers and nuns, the friendships, the space to grow—it all became the foundation that carried me through the years. I am forever grateful.

To my parents—thank you for being part of the story that made me who I am. Our journey together has shaped my resilience, my strength, and my voice.

To my siblings—whether near or far, in presence or in memory—you are part of my foundation. Through shared experiences, spoken and unspoken, you have been a part of the journey that brought me here.

To the ones who have been a part of my story, whether in presence or in spirit—thank you. To those who offered

kindness, even in small ways, your warmth lingered
longer than you may ever know.

To my younger self, who navigated the unknown with
courage—you made it. This book is proof that your effort
mattered.

To the readers who see fragments of their own story in
these words—I acknowledge your strength, your
survival, and your resilience.

And finally, to the art of poetry itself—thank you for
being a refuge, a mirror, and a voice when silence felt
safer.

The Beginning

A world—
A haven of safety,
Where fairness and mischief dance freely.
Guided by love, nurtured with care,
Shaped by discipline, yet free to explore,
Embracing the gentle uncertainty of growth...
Or so I thought it was, until...

The Background Dance

Suddenly, the nights grew long,
The days were filled with silent ache.
A place where you did not belong,
A home that made your spirit break.

At school, you found a fleeting space,
Until the night would call you back.
You hid your fears behind a face,
Pretending strength to mask the lack.

The Flower Bud

Some days felt brighter than hurt
Yet love still kept my heart strong.
Woven in moments, soft, yet plain,
Proof that family was more than pain.

The market runs, the laughs we shared,
The schoolwork help, the way they cared.
The friends, the meals, the long drives,
The love that made me feel alive.

I saw the hope, it softly shone,
and I thought, this is it-
This life, this love, this light,
I want it daily, always bright.

Kin

But then the pain returned once more,
Yet I was not alone this time.
A sibling small , my heart now swore
To shield him from the world unkind.

My fear transformed, my strength took hold,
For him, I stood up brave and tall.
Without a thought, I played the role —
A mother's love before the call.

Back then, I did not understand,
But comfort bloomed within my chest.
I kept him safe with careful hands,
Until the day I could no less.

Play

With him, I laughed in the silliest ways,
Teased and played through childhood days.
I'd boss him around, then make amends,
For in the end we were best friends.

We'd share a tub of ice cream wide,
Side by side, with joy and pride.
Late night talks and secret schemes,
Lost in our little world of dreams.

Then one day as trouble came,
He stood for me, so small, so brave.
How did he know, at such a stage,
That I needed saving from the rage?

The love, the fun, the chaos bright,
The warmth of family, pure and right.
Those moments shaped the bond we keep,
A love so strong, so vast, so deep.

But time moved on, as childhood fades,
And came a choice our parents made.
A change unknown, so hard to bear,
Yet we were young, unaware.

The Road We Didn't Choose

It was the time our fate was set,
A journey planned, yet unknown.
With nervous hearts and silent dread,
We trusted what our parents had shown.

We packed our bags, held back our fears,
Off to a place they called the best.
But as the road stretched far ahead,
A sinking truth weighed in our chests.

We reached there, unpacked, unsure,
The walls so strange, the air so new.
A place so foreign, cold and pure,
Yet nothing felt like home we knew.

Divided by Fate

We planned and plotted to fail the test,
Hoping fate would turn, give us a rest.
But nothing could defy the plan,
Our paths were set, no turning back again.

Fast forward, and time had flown,
We stood apart, yet still alone.
In different schools, we learned to cope,
One for girls, the other for hope.

Each day a step, unsure, untried,
But learning to survive with what we'd find.
Through separate halls, we carried on,
A bond so strong, though far, not gone.

What seemed to be a short escape,
Turned into fate we couldn't bend.
And how we'd stand, or how we'd fall,
Was ours to shape, ours to defend.

Learning to Stand Alone

Now began the life so real,
Where I had to stand, to think, to feel.
No turning back, no place to hide,
Strength was all I had inside.

Wake up, get dressed, show up each day,
Figure out what words to say.
Who to trust and who to fear,
How to smile, how to appear.

Then evening fell, the silence grew,
I ate, I cried, I barely knew—
Was it the mess or sinking weight?
Or fear for him in a distant place?

Strength in Helping

Slowly, I began to see,
A sense of self, a place for me.
By following rules and keeping in stride,
I made things easier, let time be my guide.

I found my strength in helping hands,
Guiding others to take a stand.
And there it was, so clear, so true—
Lifting them up made me stronger too.

The Lesson

One day, the Christian girls gathered near,
We prayed, we sang, our voices clear.
Among them stood a girl so bold,
Her words like fire, her presence cold.

Another day, a shout cut through the air,
I froze in place, consumed by fear.
I'd forgotten a needle, so small, so plain,
Yet shame had wrapped me up in pain.

Alone, I cried, in quiet despair,
Till she found me hiding there.
"If you break now, this place will win,
So stand up strong, don't give in."

I didn't grasp her words that night,
But through the years, they proved so right.
Strength was built in moments rough,
And slowly, I became enough.

Leaning on Brushstrokes

From then on, I stood up tall,
Found my peace, embraced it all.
I learned to listen, look within,
To find the strength beneath my skin.

I worked, I studied, gave my best,
Kept things in order, passed each test.
Yet one thing called beyond the rest—
A place where I could just exist.

Art, I thought, would be too much,
Perfection's weight, a heavy touch.
Yet in that space, my teacher's grace,
Turned fear into a sacred place.

A brush in hand, I felt so free,
Each stroke, a piece of healing me.
My hands would move, the hours fade,
As strokes of paint my soul conveyed.

I never knew how much I'd need
The colors, shapes, the lines to lead.
But in that place, I found release,
And art became my quiet peace.

The Freedom in Creation

Through the years, while others laughed,
Lost in shows and stories passed,
I'd sit alone, my music played,
And let my colors softly fade.

Two hours lost in painted streams,
A world beyond my quiet dreams.
With books and pens, with hues so bright,
I'd write, I'd sketch, I'd bring to life.

Pages filled and canvases grew,
A log of all I ever knew.
Even now, I feel their weight,
A past too dear to separate.

But in those moments, deep and free,
I found the truest part of me.
Without a word, without a sound,
In art and ink, my soul was found.

Becoming the Lioness

Slowly, I found myself drift away,
Lost in thought, yet firm in place.
Known by many, young and old,
A steady heart, a hand to hold.

Teachers saw what I could be,
Placed me where I failed to see.
In sports, I broke the chains of doubt,
Discovered strength I'd lived without.

Once, I shrank beneath my past,
But here, I stood, I grew so fast.
Fear still lingered, yet I dared,
Took on roles, stood prepared.

And then it came, a title grand,
More to carry, more to stand.
An office bearer, bold and free,
The school became a part of me.

Through the halls, I'd move with pride,
With quiet strength I'd lead, not hide.
No need to shout, no need to fight,
My actions roared—my silent might.

The Place that Made Me

I fell in love with all it gave,
The lessons learned, the strength it made.
It shaped me into something true,
A heart at peace, a spirit new.

To me, I was love, I was light,
Confidence soaring, steady in flight.
The fights, the drama, came and passed,
Yet peace within was built to last.

Through it all, one stood so near,
She bloomed, she thrived, with love sincere.
Still beside me, strong and bright,
A bond unshaken, pure and right.

My final year, the title came,
Head girl—pride and weight the same.
And yet, beneath the joy so vast,
Lingered whispers—this year, the last.

But love remained, the care, the grace,
The warmth of this unshaken place.
I stumbled, fell, yet rose once more,
Revived, restored like never before.

This place, my home, my guiding school,
Where life was shaped, my soul was fueled.
No words enough, no song so true—
This place is *MY BOARDING SCHOOL.*

Into the Unknown

It was time to step beyond the gate,
To carve my path, to face my fate.
Thrown into a sea so wide,
With no clear shores, no place to hide.

Adult burdens, lessons new,
A world to face, a life to choose.
Yet I glided through those early years,
Still a star, still held dear.

Teachers' pride, I shone so bright,
Yet change arrived, it dimmed my light.
The tides had turned, the storm set in,
And for a while, I drowned within.

Shelter in Storm

My first year came, the numbers vast,
A world so big, I shrank so fast.
I stepped away, I hid in shade,
No weight to bear, no roles to claim.

New faces came, so many near,
Yet none that held true friendship dear.
One remained through shifts and change,
Yet needed more than I could claim

Still, I laughed, I lived, I tried,
Held onto moments, side by side.
The years went by, the weight remained,
Adulting called, yet something stayed.

Through it all, one place was mine,
A quiet refuge, safe, divine.
For when the world felt cold, unclear,
I found my shelter—*HE was near.*

A Light Through it All

When the year had reached its end,
Friendships faded, hearts to mend.
Yet one remained, made parting light,
So I let go without a fight.

Life moved on, and love was rare,
But one left scars too deep to bear.
Still, I stood, I found my way,
A friend brought light into my days.

Another stayed through highs and lows,
A quiet strength that softly grows.
And through it all, I felt her near,
Mother Mary, calm and clear.

Her love, my anchor, ever strong,
She gave me hope to move along.
With faith to guide and light to see,
I found the strength to still be me.

The One who Knew

I sought myself, I lived, I roamed,
Chasing the youth I once had known.
Carefree laughter, joy so bright,
A life where love was my only light.

All I longed for was a place,
A love to hold, a warm embrace.
And through it all, she stood so near,
A sister's love, so strong, so clear.

In moments small, in fleeting days,
She walked with me through life's maze.
Bit by bit, she gently grew—
Until she was *the one who knew.*

Finding my Way Back

Slowly, I stepped back to see,
What family truly meant to me.
Not to turn away or run,
But to heal the past and not be undone.

They said, *stay away,* and so I did,
But not to forget, not to rid—
Instead, I learned, I made my peace,
Letting go while holding deep.

We were scattered, lost in time,
Parents busy, mountains climbed.
Siblings distant, gaps so wide,
Yet love still lived, though pushed aside.

Now we've grown, we understand,
Not perfect, yet we take a stand.
And more than giving, I've learned to receive,
To cherish myself and truly believe.

Growing

All my experiences took so much away,
Pieces of me lost along the way.
I never noticed, never knew,
How much I'd given, how much I withdrew.

Once, I gave without a doubt,
But life has shaped me inside out.
Alone, I fought, endured the weight,
Until one came and made it light.

Still, I heal, still, I grow,
Seeking peace I've yet to know.
Making space to just be free,
To find the girl I used to be.

And though the past still calls my name,
I rise above, I'm not the same.
Through every scar, through every bend,
I learn, I break, I start to mend.

The Walls that Gave Me Wings

I know now why I did what I did,
Why I fought, why I ran, why I hid.
Through every fall, I found my way,
And who I am stands tall today.

I had my faults, my reckless days,
Mistakes I made in countless ways.
I hope forgiveness finds me too,
For I was young, just passing through.

My strength came from that one space,
A shelter, a test, a sacred place.
If I could trade the world to stay,
I'd go back there without delay.

Within those walls, I learned to stand,
To face the storms with steady hands.
Boarding school, both tough and true,
Built my strength, gave me my view.

I wish to be that girl once more,
So, I take the leap, let life restore.
Grateful for the past that sings,
For those very walls—*they gave me wings.*

9 789369 532353